NANCY PELOSI

By Geoffrey M. Horn

People W... ...Know

Please visit our web site at **www.garethstevens.com.**
For a free color catalog describing our list of high-quality books,
call 1-800-542-2595 (USA) or 1-800-387-3178 (Canada). Our fax: 1-877-542-2596

Library of Congress Cataloging-in-Publication Data
Horn, Geoffrey M.
    Nancy Pelosi / by Geoffrey M. Horn.
      p. cm. — (People We Should Know)
    Includes bibliographical references and index.
    ISBN-10: 1-4339-0021-1 ISBN-13: 978-1-4339-0021-1 (lib. bdg.)
    ISBN-10: 1-4339-0162-5 ISBN-13: 978-1-4339-0162-1 (softcover)
    1. Pelosi, Nancy, 1940—Juvenile literature. 2. Legislators—United States—
Biography—Juvenile literature. 3. Women legislators—United States—Biography—Juvenile
literature. 4. United States. Congress. House—Speakers—Biography—Juvenile literature.
I. Title.
E840.8.P37H67   2009
328.73092—dc22[B]   2008043311

This edition first published in 2009 by
Gareth Stevens Publishing
A Weekly Reader® Company
1 Reader's Digest Road
Pleasantville, NY 10570-7000 USA

Copyright © 2009 by Gareth Stevens, Inc.

Executive Managing Editor: Lisa M. Herrington
Senior Editor: Brian Fitzgerald
Associate Editor: Amanda Hudson
Creative Director: Lisa Donovan
Senior Designer: Keith Plechaty
Production Designer: Cynthia Malaran
Photo Researcher: Kim Babbitt
Publisher: Keith Garton

Picture credits
Cover and title page: Richard Drew/AP Images; p. 5: AP Images; p. 6: Shutterstock; pp. 9, 10,
14, 17: Courtesy of Nancy Pelosi's office; p. 11: Courtesy of the University of Baltimore; p. 13:
Courtesy Institute of Notre Dame; p. 18: AP Images; p. 19: Corbis; p. 20: Nancy Ostertag/Getty
Images; p. 21: Arun Nevadar/Getty Images; p. 23: AP Images; p. 24: Newscom; p. 25: Dennis
Brack/Getty Images; p. 26: Mark Wilson/Getty Images; p. 28: AP Images.

Printed in the United States of America

1 2 3 4 5 6 7 8 9 10 09 08

TABLE OF CONTENTS

Words in the glossary appear in **bold** type
the first time they are used in the text.

CHAPTER 1

Madam Speaker

Bam! Bam! Bam! With three strokes of her large wooden **gavel**, Nancy Pelosi overturned more than 200 years of tradition.

Until January 2007, all 51 people who had held the title of Speaker of the **House of Representatives** were men. Other House members called them "Mister Speaker." Nancy Pelosi is the first woman ever to become Speaker. Other House members call her "Madam Speaker."

Surrounded by children, Pelosi holds up the gavel on her historic first day as Speaker of the House.

Leading Lady

As Speaker of the House, Pelosi holds a lot of power. The United States has two main political parties—the Democrats and the Republicans. Pelosi has been a Democrat all her life. The Democratic Party won a **majority** in the House in the November 2006 election. The majority gets to choose the Speaker. Pelosi's fellow representatives chose her for that important role. She had been a respected House member for nearly 20 years.

Fast Fact

The Speaker of the House ranks third among elected U.S. officials. If both the president and the vice president died in office, the Speaker would become president.

A Brief Guide to Congress

Congress has two houses: the House of Representatives and the **Senate**. Members of Congress meet in the U.S. Capitol building (left). Both houses work together to pass **bills**. Bills then become laws when the president signs them.

The House of Representatives has 435 members. Each member serves a two-year term. States with many people elect many representatives. Pelosi's home state of California elects the most members—53. States with the fewest people elect only one representative. The Senate has 100 members, two from each of the 50 states. Each senator is elected to a six-year term.

The Last Word

Nancy Pelosi has the final say over which bills the House votes on. She also controls when votes are held. She chooses which Democrats will head important House committees. She explains and defends her party's views on issues such as taxes, energy, and the environment. She meets with the president and other top officials. She also meets with foreign leaders.

Fast Fact

Pelosi won reelection in November 2008, with more than 70 percent of the vote.

History in the Making

Pelosi is not only one of the most powerful women in American history. She is also the mother of five children and grandmother of seven. When she took the gavel for the first time as Speaker, she wanted her family around her. "This is an historic moment," she said. "It's an historic moment for Congress. It's an historic moment for the women of America."

Pelosi invited the children and grandchildren of House members to gather around her. Then she banged the gavel on the desk in front of her and said, "For these children, our children, and for all of America's children, the House will come to order!"

"For our daughters and our granddaughters, now, the sky is the limit. Anything is possible for them."

–Nancy Pelosi, upon becoming Speaker of the House

Family Matters

Nancy Patricia D'Alesandro was born on March 26, 1940, in Baltimore, Maryland. She took Pelosi as her last name when she married Paul Pelosi in 1963.

Nancy's family had lots of experience in politics. In 1938, her father had won a seat in the House of Representatives. His full name was Thomas, but most people called him Tommy. When Nancy was born, Tommy was working on a House bill to provide job training for young people.

Crowds in Baltimore cheer Mayor Tommy D'Alesandro and his family, including eight-year-old Nancy, in the backseat.

Little Italy

The D'Alesandro family lived in the Little Italy section of Baltimore. Nancy's parents were Italian Americans. Nancy was named after her mother, whose full name in Italian was Annunciata. Nancy thinks her mother might have had a great career in law or business. But Tommy did not want his wife to work outside the home. In the 1940s and 1950s, most women stayed home to care for their children. "The truth is that my father and the times held her back," Nancy wrote.

Fast Fact

Pelosi is the first Italian American Speaker of the House.

This family photo shows Nancy with her parents and five older brothers.

Bending the Rules

Nancy's parents married in 1928. During the next 12 years, they had seven children. The first six were boys. One died very young. Nancy was their last child and only girl. "With all those older brothers," Nancy wrote, "I did have to find ways to hold my own."

Nancy's parents were protective of their daughter. Her parents had strict rules, such as no bike riding on the street. "I, of course, rode my bicycle on the street anyway," she said. "They got used to it—after a while."

Like Father, Like Son

One of Nancy's brothers has the same name as her father—Thomas. People called them "Little Tommy" and "Big Tommy" to tell them apart. Big Tommy was mayor of Baltimore from 1947 to 1959. Little Tommy was mayor of the same city from 1967 to 1971.

"Big Tommy" D'Alesandro

The Favor File

When Nancy was seven years old, her father became mayor of Baltimore. Many people came to the mayor with problems. He did what he could to help. So did Nancy, her mother, and her brothers.

Whenever someone called to ask for a favor, Nancy's mother wrote it down on a slip of paper. These pieces of paper were collected in a "favor file." The file listed everyone who got a favor—and anyone who could give one.

Sometimes Nancy would take phone messages from people who needed favors. "I knew exactly what Mommy would tell them," she wrote. "I heard her say it so many times."

CHAPTER 3

Finding Her Wings

Politics was important to Nancy's family. Religion was even more important. The D'Alesandros attended Saint Leo's Catholic Church in Little Italy. The church ran a school that Nancy's brothers attended.

Nancy's mother wanted something different for her daughter. As a girl, Nancy's mother had attended the Institute of Notre Dame. It was one of Baltimore's best schools. "My mother wanted to give her wings," said Nancy's brother Tommy.

The Institute of Notre Dame in Baltimore has a long history. It opened in 1847.

Learning From the School Sisters

The Institute of Notre Dame was located outside Little Italy. It attracted girls from different backgrounds. Nancy attended Notre Dame from first grade through high school.

The teachers were known as the School Sisters of Notre Dame. They trained girls to be strong leaders as well as good students. Nancy was a standout on the **debate** team. The speech skills she learned would prove very useful when she went to Congress.

A Kennedy Visit

John F. Kennedy was one of Nancy's biggest heroes when she was in high school. He was the guest of honor at a dinner in Baltimore in 1957. Nancy's father and mother were invited. Her mother stayed home and let Nancy go instead. Nancy got to sit right next to Kennedy. She had her picture taken with the young senator. Today, she proudly displays the picture in her office.

Choosing Trinity

Nancy graduated from high school in 1958. She was ready for college. Her father wanted her to choose a college in Baltimore and live at home. Again, her mother had other ideas. Both Nancy and her mother had decided on Trinity College in Washington, D.C. The school is now named Trinity Washington University. Nancy's father was not happy, but her mother stood her ground. "Poor Daddy!" Pelosi wrote later. "With Mommy as my **ally**, he didn't stand a chance."

Meeting Paul Pelosi

Nancy had a great time at Trinity. She studied history and politics. She was an active member of the College Democrats. She worked hard to get John F. Kennedy elected president in 1960. She also made a lot of friends. "My best friends from Trinity are still my best friends," she says.

Nancy also took classes at Georgetown University in Washington, D.C. There she met a tall young man from San Francisco, California. His name was Paul Pelosi, a student at Georgetown. "She was just special," Paul said later.

Love and Marriage

By Nancy's senior year, she and Paul were a couple. In 1962, Paul asked her to marry him. Their wedding took place a year later.

After they were married, Nancy and Paul moved to New York City. Paul worked as a banker. For the next six years, Nancy settled down to the work of being a full-time mom.

Fast Fact

For their first date, Paul asked Nancy out for dessert. Years later she wrote, "Paul had just stumbled across the key to my heart—chocolate."

CHAPTER 4

The Path to Power

After six years in New York City, Paul and Nancy Pelosi moved to San Francisco—his hometown—in 1969. By that time, the couple had four children: Nancy Corinne, Christine, Jacqueline, and Paul Jr. Alexandra, their fifth child, was born in 1970.

"I was a very happy young wife and mother," she wrote. "My life revolved around diapers, feeding schedules, playtime in the park, errands with babies in tow—and I loved it."

The five Pelosi children share a family moment.

Hearing the Call

Being the mother of five children kept Pelosi busy. But she never gave up her interest in politics. When Democrats needed a place to meet, she opened her home. When the Democratic Party needed money, she helped raise funds.

The mayor of San Francisco called. He knew Pelosi loved libraries. He said he could use a friendly vote on the city's library **commission**. Pelosi agreed to serve. She knew how to get things done. Word got around. Other important people began calling her for help.

California Governor Jerry Brown greets supporters in Maryland during his 1976 Democratic primary race.

Helping Jerry Brown

California Governor Jerry Brown was one of the people who asked for Pelosi's help. Brown, a Democrat, ran for president in 1976. He asked Nancy for her advice and support. Nancy didn't know him very well, but Paul did. Paul's brother had gone to high school with Brown.

Nancy urged Brown to enter a **party primary** in Maryland. Doing well in the primaries is key to becoming a party's choice for president. Pelosi worked long hours to help Brown win in the state where she was born. Her hard work paid off. Brown won the Maryland primary.

A Rising Star

Brown didn't become president. Another Democrat—Jimmy Carter—did. Still, after the election, Governor Brown praised Pelosi. With his support, she was chosen in 1977 to head the Democratic Party in northern California. Four years later, she became head of the entire state party.

The Democratic Party held its 1984 **national convention** in San Francisco. Pelosi headed the group that hosted the event. She was thrilled when Democrats picked Geraldine Ferraro as their **candidate** for vice president. Ferraro was the first woman named by a major party to run for vice president. It was a historic moment—even though Ferraro lost the November election.

Geraldine Ferraro waves to friends and fans in 1984.

Running for Congress

Early in 1987, Pelosi visited her friend Sala Burton. Sala's husband, Phil, had served 19 years in Congress. When Phil died in 1983, Sala took his seat in the House of Representatives. Now Sala was dying, and she wanted Pelosi to run for her seat.

Pelosi was stunned. She hadn't planned to run for Congress—at least not yet. She needed to talk with her family.

Nancy's Children

Several of Nancy Pelosi's children have become well known. Like his father, Paul Pelosi Jr. went into business. He is also interested in helping the environment. Like her mother, Christine Pelosi is very active in politics. One of her main jobs is helping Democrats who want to run for Congress. Alexandra Pelosi (left) makes films. Her movies about politics and religion have been shown on TV.

Paul and Nancy Pelosi attend an event at the Kennedy Center in Washington, D.C.

A Family Decision

In her book *Know Your Power*, Pelosi describes what happened after Sala asked her to run for Congress. She asked her husband, who said it was all right with him. Then she asked her youngest daughter, Alexandra, who was still in high school. She told her daughter she would need to be away from home a lot. "I know this is a big deal, so if you don't want me to do it, I won't," she said.

Alexandra gave her approval. Once Pelosi had her family on board, there was nothing holding her back.

CHAPTER 5

Taking Charge

In 1987, Pelosi won a special election to the House of Representatives. A year later, she was elected to a full two-year term. People in San Francisco have been reelecting her ever since. She usually wins by a large margin.

When Pelosi first entered Congress, the subject she cared most about was **AIDS**. Many people in San Francisco had already died of the disease. Pelosi became a leader in the fight against AIDS. She worked to make sure that people who had AIDS were treated with respect. She has also worked hard on women's and children's health issues.

Pelosi shares the excitement at her San Francisco headquarters in 1987.

Moving Up

Pelosi spoke out on matters that were important to her. She also knew how to work the system. She gained support for her causes by helping other members of Congress with their causes. Because she was so popular in her district, she could afford to spend time helping other party members in tougher races. In turn, those members supported her when she needed their votes.

Fast Fact

When Pelosi went to Congress in 1987, there were 23 women in the House. By 2008, the number had risen to 75.

In Congress, Pelosi has often worked closely with the president. In this 1993 photo, she looks on as President Bill Clinton signs an order to boost trade with China.

Making History

In 2001, Pelosi became Democratic **whip**. She was the first woman in the House to hold that title. The whip's job is to make sure members vote the way party leaders want them to.

Pelosi broke new ground a year later. In the House, each party has a leader. Democrats elected her House **minority leader** in 2002. She was the first woman to lead a party in Congress.

Four years later, Democrats won a majority in the House. They got to choose the Speaker for the first time in 12 years. For Democrats, Pelosi was the clear and historic choice.

A Cause for Celebration

Over the years, Pelosi has had her disagreements with Republicans. But on the day she became Speaker, they joined in the applause.

On January 4, 2007, Republican leader John Boehner handed Pelosi the gavel. Just about everyone on the House floor stood up and cheered.

Sandra Day O'Connor

Historic Firsts

This time line lists some important firsts for women in politics.

1866: Elizabeth Cady Stanton is the first woman to run for the U.S. House of Representatives, even though she is not allowed to vote.

1917: Jeannette Rankin of Montana is the first woman to win election to the U.S. House of Representatives.

1920: Women gain the right to vote in elections throughout the United States.

1968: Shirley Chisholm of New York becomes the first African American woman elected to the House.

1981: Sandra Day O'Connor is the first woman appointed to the U.S. Supreme Court.

1984: Geraldine Ferraro, a congresswoman from New York, is the first woman chosen by a major party to run for vice president.

2007: Nancy Pelosi is the first woman to serve as Speaker of the House.

The 100 Hour Plan

When Pelosi became Speaker, House Democrats came up with the "100 Hour Plan." During the first few weeks of January 2007, they would pass laws that would help workers, students, and other Americans.

Speaker Pelosi greets President George W. Bush in 2007.

To help millions of workers, Pelosi wanted to raise the **minimum wage**. The minimum wage is the lowest amount of money a company can pay its workers. On January 10, the House passed a bill to increase the minimum wage to $7.25 an hour by 2009. The Senate agreed. In May, President George W. Bush signed the bill.

Pelosi pushed to make college more affordable. On January 17, the House approved a bill to make college loans easier to pay back. President Bush signed the bill in September.

The Road Ahead

Pelosi faced some disappointments. When she became Speaker, the United States had 132,000 troops in Iraq. House Democrats wanted to start pulling U.S. forces out of Iraq. President Bush and many other Republicans opposed that idea. The number of U.S. forces in Iraq went up.

By the fall of 2008, the U.S. economy was in serious trouble. Some large banks went out of business. Other banks lowered the amount of money they lent to people. Food and gas prices were high. The number of people without jobs continued to increase. Pelosi tried to work with President Bush and with other Republicans in Congress to keep the problems from getting worse.

Fast Fact

Pelosi was the chairperson of the Democratic National Convention in August 2008.

66Work for what you believe in, whether it's on a local, state, or national level.99

—Nancy Pelosi

Pelosi hopes to help President Barack Obama solve some of the nation's problems.

New Goals

Despite these huge challenges, Pelosi remains hopeful. She looks forward to working with President Barack Obama. He is a Democrat and the first African American to be elected president.

Pelosi knows the road ahead will be tough. But she continues to believe that "America should work for everyone—not just the privileged few." She says, "We have made history. Now, let us make progress."

Time Line

1940 — Nancy Patricia D'Alesandro is born on March 26 in Baltimore, Maryland.

1947 — Nancy's father, Thomas (Tommy) D'Alesandro, is elected mayor of Baltimore.

1962 — Nancy graduates from Trinity College in Washington, D.C.

1963 — Nancy marries Paul Pelosi on September 7. From 1964 to 1970, they have five children.

1969 — The Pelosi family moves from New York City to San Francisco, California.

1981 — Nancy becomes the head of the Democratic Party in California.

1987 — Nancy wins her first election to the U.S. House of Representatives.

2007 — On January 4, Nancy is sworn in as the first female Speaker of the House.

Glossary

AIDS: a disease that weakens the body's natural ability to fight other diseases; short for "acquired immune deficiency syndrome"

ally: a supporter; a friend

bills: written plans for a new law to be considered by Congress

candidate: a person who is running for office

commission: a group of people chosen to perform some official duty

debate: a formal discussion in which two sides argue opposing points of view

gavel: a type of mallet or hammer, which the Speaker bangs on the desk to bring the House to order

House of Representatives: a house of Congress, with 435 voting members elected to two-year terms

majority: more than half

minimum wage: the lowest amount an employer can pay employees

minority leader: the leader of the minority party in the House

national convention: a large gathering at which a political party officially announces its candidate for president

party primary: a state election in which members of a political party vote for their candidate for president

Senate: a house of Congress, with 100 voting members elected to six-year terms

whip: the party leader in the House who gets members to vote the way the leadership team wants them to

Find Out More

Books

Gutman, Howard. *The Speaker of the House*. America's Leaders. Farmington Hills, Mich.: Blackbirch Press, 2003.

Thimmesh, Catherine. *Madam President: The Extraordinary, True (and Evolving) Story of Women in Politics*. New York: Sandpiper, 2008.

Thomas, William David. *What Are the Parts of Government?* My American Government. Pleasantville, N.Y.: Gareth Stevens, 2008.

Web Sites

Ben's Guide to U.S. Government for Kids
www.bensguide.gpo.gov

Congress for Kids
www.congressforkids.net/index.htm

Speaker Nancy Pelosi—Kids' Page
www.speaker.house.gov/kids

Source Notes

pp. 7, 28: "Rep. Nancy Pelosi's Remarks Upon Becoming Speaker of the House." WashingtonPost.com. January 4, 2007. www.washingtonpost.com/wp-dyn/content/article/2007/01/04/AR2007010401039.html

pp. 9, 10, 11, 14, 15 (Fast Fact), 16, 21, 27: Pelosi, Nancy with Amy Hill Hearth. *Know Your Power*. New York: Doubleday, 2008.

p. 12: Bzdek, Vincent. *Woman of the House*. New York: Palgrave Macmillan, 2008.

p. 15 (top): "Trinity Graduates Win Re-election." www.trinitydc.edu. November 8, 2006. www.trinitydc.edu/news_events/2006/1007_pelosi.php

p. 15 (center): Sandalow, Marc. *Madam Speaker: Nancy Pelosi's Life, Times, and Rise to Power*. New York: Modern Times, 2008.

Index

About the Author

Geoffrey M. Horn has written more than three dozen books for young people and adults, along with hundreds of articles for encyclopedias and other works. He lives in southwestern Virginia, in the foothills of the Blue Ridge Mountains, with his wife, their collie, and six cats. He dedicates this book to the children—Amelia, Harry, Emily, Jacob, and Sophia.